FROM MASCARA TO MANHOOD

ISBN: 9781700500953

A publication of Tall Pine Books || An imprint of Pulpit to Page
TALLPINEBOOKS.COM || PULPITTOPAGE.COM

*Printed in the United States of America

FROM MASCARA TO MANHOOD

BENJAMIN BLAKE HOWARD

Tall Pine

"I had the privilege of watching Blake walk out this beautiful journey of restoration. This is a message that speaks deep into the heart of a generation, crying out for a revelation of their true identity. Through the pages of this book, Blake invites you to join him on a journey that will lead you to the only One who holds the answer to the deepest questions of *who we really are.*"

— KAREN WHEATON
THE RAMP

"Blake's testimony is truly amazing. I have personally seen the transformation in his life over the years and his story is a testimony to the life transforming power of God!"

— JACOB PETERSON
JACOB PETERSON MINISTRIES

"Raw, real, eye-opening, and life changing! In this beautiful testimony, Blake exposes the beliefs that kept his mind and heart in a prison of uncertainty and pain. It is a *must read* for anyone who is on the road to finding who they are. This book shines a light on how God views the LGBTQ community and how we as a church body have to change to truly love and reach them."

— LINDSEY DOSS
HOPE UNLIMITED

To My Beautiful Wife, you are my rock and I will never stop pursuing you.

To my Family, thank you for always supporting me and loving me through my journey.

CONTENTS

1

LETTING GO OF "HER"

Ephesians 1:5 (ESV) "He predestined us for adoption to himself as sons through Jesus Christ, according to the purpose of his will."

AS THE TITLE SUGGESTS, this is a true story of a transition, and as the above scripture suggests, it's about identity. This transition I mention happened in a guy's life a few years ago, and it caused the identity he had held to be wiped away and made new. This guy met someone who absolutely changed his life, and when he met that someone he decided to change his life and let go of who he thought he was and grab hold of who he was to become. Now this is not some lousy, cheesy relationship story about someone who, in order to win the love of another, changed who they were completely, but it *is* a story about a *change*. This is the story of a guy who was caught up in a LGBTQ world that he never really belonged in. But before we go too far, let's back up a little.

Let's get some backstory. Our leading man grew up in a home with Christian values, where smoking, drinking and cussing were wrong and to talk about the "G-word" was out of the question. For awhile he only got what bit of *worldly knowledge* he had from his older friends in the neighborhood, but he never had enough to put two and two together about much of anything. One day he experienced a change. This event pushed him even further towards seeing boys differently. He began fantasizing as early as ten years old about men, the way that only adults should fantasize. These ideas intrigued him and as he grew he pursued them in different ways, but never as a full-blown gay relationship.

For a majority of his teen life our guy was gay. Closeted...but gay. He never truly connected to the men in his life so it was hard for him to see himself as the man he was supposed to be. Unfortunately another guy took what innocence he had away from him at a young age and this made him very confused even as a child. He had never really learned "How to Be a Guy" and had always hung with his "Besties for the resties" girl friends. There wasn't an instruction guide on "Being a Guy," so he was at a loss. He also had never had a boyfriend but had tried to date girls. His parents were everything to him and he didn't want to ruin their reputation or the family name they had built for themselves by *coming out*.

They attended a mega church, were Christian, and he wanted to live up to their standards for his life. He wanted to show them that he could measure up to what was expected of him and be the perfect son. Although his mother and father both supported him in everything he did, he always felt he had to win the affection and approval of his father. He had compared himself to his brother for so long he thought his parents wanted him to be just as perfect as he thought his sibling was. His mother worked hard to love and support him at home while his father worked hard at earning a living for them to live a wonderful and abundant life. As time passed he graduated high school and still lived *under the radar*. He had been able to *stay in the closet*. Except for the bullying and rumors people told, he had his friends convinced he was straight. There were a few bumps and run-ins with other gay guys but he fizzled them out. Unfortunately as most stories have a plot twist, the first twist in this story hit hard.

This guy fell in love. He fell in love with a guy that he wished and hoped would one day be his Prince Charming. He fell in love with the idea of love and let it carry him on a journey that felt endless. After seven to nine months of an on and off commitment, and a blurred perception of "bliss" with his boyfriend, he fell out of love. The two guys broke up and never dated again. Heartbroken and depressed, our leading man went rouge. He began hooking up with people right and left and felt his life spinning out of control. Then he met "Her." This dark and mysterious façade that he never knew was there.

He had always been fascinated with women and the power he saw they had, and deep inside, he wanted to be one. In theatre he had learned the ropes of drag, how to properly wear heels and highlighter, and the ways of the trade. One night "She" was born. The guy went to the nearest makeup counter and dropped $180 on the basics needed to produce the woman he named "Velma." She was his darker side and was what he thought he had wanted all his life. On the side of the hookups and false lashes, he was also hooked on weed and had access to plenty of money to spend on the things "Velma" required.

Our guy hid her from just about everyone and only a few people knew about her. After a few appearances "Velma's" career became short lived. Her eyelashes, contour and rougé didn't seem to fill the void that this guy still had. He loved the attention but hated that "Velma" got the attention instead of him. So then, he put her away. He locked her in the dungeon of his heart and kept her confined there. However, she still had control of his mindset. Now what? Who or what was he? All he wanted was to marry a nice guy have two kids and live happily ever after.

But was that really what he wanted? He decided that he was going to fulfill the female role he thought he wanted and was going to raise kids. He had helped so much with his older brother's kids that he felt he understood the challenges and he thought it would be easy. He felt that he was SUPPOSED to fill this void with his female desires and really considered adopting at 19. That plan wasn't realistic, he discovered, and so the idea quickly died.

Still, he played this womanly façade everywhere he went, even though "Velma" was out of the picture. With the few guy friends he had, in his head he pretended to be the *girl best friend* and tried to give them everything they needed. Serving them as if they were his man.

Time passed and he pushed *who he thought he was* out of the way. But he realized even in progressing relationships with girls, he still wanted to play the *leading female* in the scene. He wasn't about to let someone else take the lead. The confusion of what he really wanted in life was all a blur, so he decided to relax about it for awhile. For now all he had left were parties and "good times" so he went with it. He was done searching.

He had some close friends that he smoked weed with regularly and that progressed into trying cocaine for the first time. Almost every night they would snort up 2-4 lines each of intoxicating coke and then see what cards the never-ending night dealt. After a month he began tiptoeing the line of overdosing on cocaine. It shook him up a little. He then vowed he would never snort another line. For a moment he thought that the drugs made the confusion about whom he wanted to sleep with at night go away, but it didn't. The moment he sobered up, BOOM! There were his endless thoughts again.

At this point you may be wondering, "Does this story even have a happy ending?"

Well it does...for this guy.

For "Velma" and her controlling mind games...not so much.

This guy decided that "if everything that world has to offer brings me never-ending emptiness, then why continue to pursue it?" He had heard about these Christian colleges and honestly thought they were a joke, but at this point was willing to try anything. Maybe he could find a nice Christian school where he could get a college education and fly under the radar again. He had considered himself a "Liberal Christian" and thought that maybe this was a good option to stay away from drugs, alcohol and "Velma." But there was another school his mother had suggested. It was a school where his cousin attended and he knew they wouldn't approve of him. He was nervous about it considering he was still gay and he knew if ANYONE found out, he'd be back in the small world of Georgia.

He applied, not thinking he would get in, but a day later he was accepted. He told his mom he'd try it, knowing it would be hell. He decided to give up dreams of being a performer and move to Alabama where he attended his first casual church service in awhile. It had been a year or two since he'd actually cared about keeping up with church and so it was a bit awkward. It was the day before orientation and he was still hesitant. But he was there and he decided that if God were all He was cracked up to be, he would at least try Him out. He instantly felt a real presence in the room and got lost in worship.

Song after song he gave it his all, dancing and singing like everyone around him. Then he met that Someone, and that Someone caused his life to change forever. It was the REAL Jesus. He had never experienced Him in this way and completely let go of all of his baggage. The drugs and alcohol seemed like ridiculous shortcuts when compared to the wonder of Jesus. Jesus met him and wiped away the drunken nights, the lines of cocaine and the one-night stands. It was in an instant that the voids, one right after the other, were filled. He opened his heart and let "Velma," along with a lot of other binding identities, free to be melted by the light of Jesus.

This began a new chapter of a journey that had just begun. Now our leading guy began to let go of "her."

This idea that he was to fulfill the role of a female and everything that came with it. He let the drugs go. He let the alcohol go. He let "Her" Go. Now he felt a freedom but this was only the beginning. The next chapter-of this story is just another piece to his story.

2

THE MORNING AFTER

WELL BY NOW YOU may wonder who this guy is. Who was the guy trapped in the heels, and bound by a false identity. It's me. I was the one that strove for attention and had no sense of identity. For me false lashes, rougé and contour could never hide the blemishes of my identity. But now everything had changed. *I had changed!* He changed me, but what now? It was the morning after and I wasn't sure what was next.

That next week came and I began this journey of learning to be a man, but not just a man, a *man of God.* Being a man can mean so much more than what we perceive as "being a man." For me, I not only was gay, but I also had a female complex that kept me from seeing light in any other area. In no way does being gay make you less of a man, for me I just wanted to be some man's perfect wife. What the world has taught men they should be is not what God called us to be. Being a man can't be taught in a short school session or on the playground.

Yet I didn't even know what being a man looked like so I wasn't sure how long it took. By this time in my life, looking at the men in my life as *examples* seemed impossible. I started to consider what my life looked like from here and I drew a blank. I honestly never felt I could be with a man without my family and friends deserting me, but being with women seemed so foreign to me at this point. I knew that whatever I felt in that service though, was so real and deep, I couldn't live without it.

As a few months went on I began developing a relationship with Jesus. Every other day for at least 30 minutes I was praying and talking to Him, just as I would any other friend. Sometimes I didn't know what I was doing at all so most of the time it was just me asking questions to God and waiting for answers. The God I had experienced was actually real. He spoke with me and listened to me and helped me consistently. I was so amazed that I had stumbled on a *real God*, or rather He had found ME. I had never experienced anything like this before. But this is where I began falling short.

As I mentioned to you in the previous anecdote I struggled with same sex attraction and the mindset of a female. Now before, I never considered this a "struggle" because it was my life. But now that I was serving God, it got in the way of everything I was supposed to believe. I couldn't go into a room without checking out the guys and deciding in my head, which were the best looking ones. I felt confused and scared because I had found a life worth pursuing yet I wasn't doing it right. I had moved to school in Alabama, but the big kicker was *I lived with guys.* I lived with five other guys actually, and it stressed me out. I never wanted to be home and I purposefully caused friction to create a barrier, and for the first time I was scared of being attracted to guys. I didn't know what else to do but hate them. I had never been in this position before and I didn't feel comfortable in my dorm house. My mind and my heart were swirling and I felt like it was a battle. Then one day I came across this...

Psalms 24:3-5 (ESV) "Who shall ascend the hill of the LORD? And who shall stand in his holy place? He who has clean hands and a pure heart, who does not lift up his soul to what is false and does not swear deceitfully. He will receive blessing from the LORD and righteousness from the God of his salvation."

I had been pursuing God without checking my mind and my heart. I didn't know what to do next. I was lost. If I was truly supposed to be gay then how was I supposed to pursue God with all of my heart if I was still pursuing men with my entire mind? But if I wasn't meant to be

gay how was I supposed to just "stop liking guys" altogether. I was at a loss. I had really just decided to
manage both, be a Gay Liberal Christian and find
people that accepted me that way. That December I
went to a conference in Tennessee to serve the ministry
where I was attending school.

About the second night of the conference, the lead
pastor of the church preached. His message was incredible and something about it gripped me and I broke.
Something that man said gripped me so deep I turned to
God and I said, "I'll live for you and I refuse to be gay
any more!" Easier said than done, but that was the twist.
I DIDN'T want that life anymore and so it became
something that actually sounded doable. The next few
months I prayed and I had quiet time with God and I
tried to focus on other things but I still dealt with same
sex attraction. I was upset. I had spent so much time
pursuing God and yet the desire for guys had not left
me; I still wanted to meet one in my bed late at night.

Then as the season progressed into summer, and the
end of my first year in ministry school, I decided I
needed to have men of God in my life to show me what
to do and to help me out of where I was. I actually
started connecting with some of the guys in my house
and then I became brothers with one in particular. We
ended up living together for school and again the next
year. I began to learn so much from him. Together we
pushed and helped prune each other, in a sense, so our

qualities and gifts that God had given us would be drawn out to shine. I connected with a couple of leaders who stepped in and became a brother and a father figure to me. They helped me and walked with me to continue to run after God the way I should. But with all of this I still was left just a bit confused. Even though I was getting so much information and help spiritually, I still felt that urge to be physical with a man. One day in class one of my professors had mentioned "having a changed heart sometimes means having changed surroundings."

Psalm 119:37 (ESV) "Turn my eyes from looking at worthless things; and give me life in your ways."

It made so much sense. What I surrounded myself with was what I would constantly think about. So I filtered what I watched and listened to and I began seeing my issues and mind games fading. For example, I stopped watching the certain dating shows that promoted men in a sexual way. I altogether stopped watching things that included sexual connotations of men. I stopped listening to songs that promoted sex and lust or things I listened to in the past to make me feel "naughty."

After a few months of this, I felt better and it was so much easier to go into a room full of guys. I found myself daydreaming of marriage and kids still, but now my daydreams didn't include a *husband.* I no longer walked around ashamed. I could be proud of myself because I started seeing a change. It began a whole new concept of *Happily Ever After*. But what I didn't consider is how hard it would be to put up a fight.

3

IT TAKES MORE THAN MASCARA

THE FIGHT. It's probably one of the toughest things I've ever gone through. It takes more than a waterproof mascara to get you through something like this. Guarding your eyes is a daily decision that we all must make regardless of what we come from. To someone who has come from a life of alcoholism it can be hard just to be in a room full of friends and family drinking a beer. The same goes for coming from a homosexual life.

Scrolling through social media and all of the sudden, there he is, a sweaty guy at the gym getting in his daily gym post. You look. Move on. Now you can't stop thinking about him. What he looks like. Then you scroll back up. You start zooming. Then you go to his account and scroll through his pictures. Then somehow you make your way to a porn site of guys in a gym hooking up. It's the simplest thing, a picture, but it can lead right

down into a path of temporary pleasure and false satis-
factions.

For me I had to decide to un-follow these types of
guys and accounts that did nothing but promote themselves sexually. Some of them were close friends and
people I cared about, some were just random people I
followed because they were attractive. It was something
I had to do. Having these men in front of me all the time
only peaked my sexual drive and not my longing for the
things of God.

> Proverbs 4:23-27 (ESV) "Keep your heart with all
> vigilance, for from it flow the springs of life. Put away
> from you crooked speech, and put devious talk far from
> you. Let your eyes look directly forward, and your gaze
> be straight before you. Ponder the path of your feet;
> then all your ways will be sure. Do not swerve to the
> right or to the left; turn your foot away from evil."

For me, when I fell in love with Jesus it was like
falling head over heels for someone you'll spend the rest
of your life with. When you find someone like that you
would do anything for him or her. Give up things, make
compromises, and it's the same thing for Him. I wanted
to cut those things out so I wasn't tempted. It's a give and
receive relationship. The simplest task of guarding my
eyes and mind was so minuscule that I was willing to do
anything to make that happen. Just as the Book of

Proverbs mentions, you must be careful where you let you mind go because it helps run your life. It honestly blew my mind how much just the simplest things could lead you to such betrayal. Now that I had this whole concept of guarding myself I felt like I was finally getting somewhere. Unfortunately though, somewhere between the train station and my destination I forgot one big thing. My foundation.

4

FULL-COVERAGE FOUNDATION

YOU WOULD THINK any good queen would remember *with any great thing you need a good foundation,* but I never thought that would apply to this. It had been the answer behind it all. As many of you at this point are probably wondering "what does he mean by foundation?" or maybe the thought has entered your head "I've experienced God but *nothing,* why am I different" or "I know God, but I still like guys...maybe it's God's choice for me to be gay."

Maybe it's time to ask yourself, *"Do I really know God?"* or *"Am I so one with God I know who He really is...or who I really am?"* These were the real questions I had to ask myself. I had to be blunt and real in knowing Him. For me, even after all the wonderful and meaningful encounters I had, that I have previously described to you, I needed something more. The answers to those questions were "No." I hadn't really gotten to KNOW God. I didn't know Him so well I knew who He really was and is. I needed firm foundation, and not a Honey Beige W2.

Not having a foundation, and basing your walk with God on an *encounter,* rather than *a consistent relationship,* will cause you to fall into the darkest of dance routines: The *Relapse Rumba.* It begins with a simple yes to a thought, or a yes to looking at a promiscuous picture. The simplest thing can send you into a relapse. That's what happened to me. I was basing my walk with God on my Sunday and Wednesday church services and not carving out time just to be with God. I walked and talked like a follower of Christ but my heart wasn't there. I began walking down a path of darkness and shadows. I began being shaded from the light that was there to clean me of my faults and insecurities. Then it happened. I cheated.

Now I wasn't in a relationship, but yet I did cheat. I cheated on the One that calls me *Beloved.* Jesus. I had somehow decided that the One who sculpted the earth and the stars wasn't great enough to fix me. I turned to one that had brought me pleasure before. The one that I had unfortunately let hold my heart for too long. And there we met and "went out to talk and catch up." We reminisced, we laughed and to no surprise I convinced myself he was still the one for me. The night ended in darkness and regret. He walked away satisfied and feeling great. I was left there hurting, full of regret, and wondering how I went from being on fire for God to back in the bed I laid in before.

Now, through my dramatic language I hope you gathered I slept with my ex and it was a terrible mistake. After being overly dramatic and bawling my eyes out for an hour I looked up to God, and I prayed a prayer that I'm sure someone has probably prayed at some point. "God, what happened? Where did it all go wrong? Why did I sleep with him AGAIN? Why can't I get out and leave this feeling? Jesus, I need you. I need to feel you again and not this dark emptiness I have." It was then that I felt the Almighty God move His presence into my room and change everything that wasn't pure. It honestly moved me so much that even when I wasn't faithful to God He was faithful to me. In a moment He came down to my bed of sin and scooped me up like a little boy. He dusted me off and clothed me in His mercy and sat me back up again. Like a father. This had been the key to having a foundation with Him that I had been missing all this time, *having a Father-Son relationship.*

Having a father-son relationship had been what I was missing this entire time. It had been a little difficult because I had never had a lot in common with my earthly father, and although he was there for me, I still chose not to bond with my father. To see God as a true father, was difficult. Just as my other seasons, God helped me move through this one as well. I began to have a relationship with Him and not just a Sunday/Wednesday prayer request and worship session. I just started to talk. Consistently. We would laugh and I would cry. We talked about where I was and how far I had come and how far I could go. He gave me revelation of Him and His love and His many other qualities and I began to feel whole. He also showed me why it had been so hard.

> Matthew 7:21-23 (ESV) "Not everyone who says to me, 'Lord, Lord,' will enter the kingdom of heaven, but the one who does the will of my Father who is in heaven. On that day many will say to me, 'Lord, Lord, did we not prophesy in your name, and cast out demons in your name, and do many mighty works in your name?' And then will I declare to them, 'I never knew you; depart from me, you workers of lawlessness.'"

As I was praying one evening I found this. As I read it over and over, the fear of God fell on me. I realized this whole time I hadn't been getting to know God. Even though I had finally opened up and began to be more consistent with Him, I wasn't being relational. I wasn't taking the time to seek who He is. So then I made the decision. "God, I'll give you everything. I'll give up hobbies, I'll give up my movies and media, and I'll give up boys. If I'm going to be able to say I tried God I want to say I tried God full force...if I don't see change and want to turn back...I will." It was a process to get where I felt Him everyday whether or not I asked Him to be there, but it happened.

He was always with me and I could actually feel His tangible presence around me. As time moved on I began seeing more and more change for me on the horizon. I saw myself changing and it scared me. I wasn't sure if I was really ready for such a change. In the past when I felt people wanted me to change or conform I blocked them to protect myself so I could stay who I thought I was. This way I could continue to hide in this safe closet I never belonged in. So I began blocking God in certain areas. In a sense I was now receiving through a thick filter rather then fully getting everything God had for me.

5

YOU'VE BEEN BLOCKED

NOW HERE'S where things got messy. For me, as many tears as I cried, I thought I had suffered the most. That wasn't so. Blocking the hand of God in my life was actually making things harder. I wanted with everything in me to fully pursue Him, but I was scared. I wasn't sure that letting Him fully change me was what I wanted. I had done the same to my family before I started following Jesus and it felt like history was repeating itself. I thought I had truly suffered because I lived in a world where no one could accept me for who I was (a gay drag queen) and no one truly supported me.

This was kind of was where I was with God, because even after God had changed some things in me and about me I began to get to a point where I thought, "why can't God just accept me for who I am?" I felt I was doing enough and if God loved me why did He demand so much of me? By blocking these people that were simply trying to help, or just be there for me, I was keeping them from actually helping me out of the darkness I was in. I realized my family suffered more than I did just by the decision I made to block them out.

I want you to stop and think of people that you may have blocked out or built a wall against. Whether it's your family, or close friends, or even God. It's so important to stop and look at the intentions of those people because sometimes we can lose them in our own selfish agendas. Sometimes our decisions affect others more than we know because all they wanted to do was help us in the first place. I personally was always frustrated and defensive with my parents, my brother, and his wife. When it came to interacting with them, I just came off as mean and heartless. I was standoffish and always filled with attitude because I didn't want to change for them.

I wanted love and acceptance, yet all I gave them were cold shoulders and heartless remarks. I had them under conditions and standards they couldn't meet. It wasn't because I hated my family and wanted nothing to do with them, but it was because I built a wall to block out the people who I felt wouldn't accept the person that I felt I really was. Later, I tried to do the same with God. I began to build walls so I could control how much God could change me, and in what areas. I have news. *God wants it all.* He wants to leave His signature on every part of your life so you can resemble Him.

I never *came out* to my parents, because I thought with the southern Christian roots that still flowed through their veins; I would never be accepted and could possibly be kicked out of my own home. Even though that would have never happened, I still believed it and I blocked them out. The next two on my black list were my brother and his wife. Although for a while I used their home and love as a safe haven from the cold lonely world I lived in, I still didn't fully let them see the real me.

I remember a night they thought they caught me in my mess, but really only had only seen a glimpse of what was happening in my life. They confronted me about smoking weed based on some things they found on my computer and we had a whole discussion about it. I felt like I was being attacked and it became more of an argument, but in reality I wanted to argue about something else. I wanted them to confront me about living a homosexual lifestyle or catch me as a drag queen, so I could prove them wrong. Prove that the life I was secretly living was truly for me.

Blocking people out simply because you are scared of what they think or even just simply because you are afraid to hurt them with the truth is only hurting those people more. It also does more damage to you. For those that feel pushed out, we are sorry. We are truly, deeply and sincerely sorry. It's so easy for us to push you away because we think we are protecting you or ourselves, but it is a lie we tell ourselves so we can get through our own lives. We are sorry for the things we said about you no matter how much you cared for us. For those doing the pushing, God doesn't hide from us because He thinks it will be better for us to heal without Him.

He comes in and messes up everything we have just so He can be in everything. He wants to be there through every step. We sometimes tend to have a mind-set, especially coming out of a homosexual lifestyle, that everyone is against us. Even God. This isn't true, without inviting God to move in us and heal us and change us we can't expect to get any closer to Him. We have to be okay with Him changing what we have had for so long so we can see how much better everything is with Him. For a time when I was in early pursuit of God, sometimes things started to get messed up and I felt I was changing so I would block God out.

This way I could stay who I was and where I was at just a little longer. In reality we can't block God out. We have to let Him come in and continue changing us so we can be more like Him in every area of our lives and see all the improvement He has made in our lives. With the world's mindset, making any change has to be this huge process of redefining identity. Not only does the change have to be our decision, but we also have to be in complete control and it can only really benefit us. When others try to come in and help us, we feel they are just here to change us and it's considered abuse. It's taking away who we are as an individual, even if it is for our good. We can't just accept that maybe things really do have to change.

> Romans 12:2 (NLT) "Don't copy the behavior and customs of this world, but let God transform you into a new person by changing the way you think. Then you will learn to know God's will for you, which is good and pleasing and perfect."

We have to let God transform us. It's not because He doesn't like us for who we are, because God made us who we are, but when we grow and move through life without Him, we become more like the world and less and less like the Father who created us in His own image. When this happens we must go on a journey to seek the roots from which we came and to let Him bring us back home. Blocking God or those people who love us, who may even be praying for us, is the last thing we must do.

It is through their prayers and love that we can see the love of Jesus and through God's movement we begin to get a better picture of what He wants for us in this world. As I began to get a grasp of this concept I became more and more able to see the things God wanted to change were for my overall well being. It seems so silly to me now that I look back and think *why did I ever put up so many walls?* But at the time it felt like the safest thing to do. I now challenge you to text, message or even call those people that perhaps you blocked. Not just for you, but for your future and theirs. Mend those relationships and allow God to mend you. If coming out of a homo-sexual lifestyle is something you desire or are consider-ing, then this step is one of the most important.

I will say this, there will NEVER be anyone in the LGBTQ community that will tell you that you can change back, or decide you made the wrong decision, or decide you want something better. I will also tell you this. Putting up walls and putting up barriers only hurts you and the people around you and it truly is a mind game the world has let you play. You're hurt, so you block out people. Rather than: you're hurt so you get help and advice.

It's a scary world out there and coming out of any lifestyle, whether you're gay, an alcoholic, a druggie, a gang member or you've been cheating on your spouse; we have to let people in and let God in to move forward. I'm here to tell my story because I haven't wanted to go back. I have never found a point with God that it was just worth giving up. As I mentioned earlier, I told God I would give Him a chance, and breaking down the walls was a part of this process. Yes things may get hard and you feel like you want to give up, but then God begins to immediately remind you of how good He really is. When we block Him out, it takes longer to get to this realization.

6

A BROTHER TO LOVE

AT THIS POINT I was everywhere. After realizing that I had to cut out shows and songs, I wondered what else I would have to cut out. I had never been *just friends* with any guys and I felt honestly, that was for the best. I was cutting out things that promoted men so why should I connect with men, if that was my issue. When I first began this journey, after allowing Jesus to change me, I was against being around guys. I lived in a house with five other guys my first year of schooling and I was always afraid if I took the time to get to know them, I'd be attracted to them. I'd spent 24/7 with my cousin, avoiding male contact, so bonding with guys just wasn't on my to-do list.

This was a lie from the enemy though. God created us as relational creatures in order for us to help each other and commune with one another. Going to ministry school I had multiple leaders wanting to pour into me, but because they were men, I was scared to open up. I had plenty of opportunity to connect and make friends with the guys in my class but I stayed so closed. I was convinced that the minute I opened up, they would judge me or look at me differently or even be afraid of me being attracted to them. As Proverbs says, "A brother is born to help in time of need" and until that point, it never occurred to me that I could have brothers in the guys around me. I see this piece of truth in two ways. I have found that not only do you need brothers to run beside you, but also brothers that will grab your hand and lead you through the wilderness. These things I learned and still grasp tightly today. This season of learning to be a brother truly allowed me to learn how much I had missed with my own brother.

As I previously mentioned, I blocked him and my father out to the place that even when they attempted to bond and grow with me, I held them at bay. The truth is, I didn't lack a male role model to follow, I simply chose not to go that path. Gravitating towards the women and female friends in my life just seemed easier. As that summer hit and I was transitioning to my second year of schooling, I felt that I needed to connect with a leader at my school. I had set up a meeting with one in particular and began meeting with him a couple of times every so often. On one occasion he directly asked me if I had struggled with same sex-attraction, and I lied straight to his face and said no. He always kept interest in me, even though I pushed him away and I finally realized he really just wanted to help me.

I remember the first time I sat in his office and all I could do was spill my guts to him. I told him I struggled for so long with same sex-attraction and I was at a point where I just needed a male leader in my life and I felt like God had chosen him. From there on I began serving him and his family in every way I could and I continued to progress. It finally occurred to me that after everything I had done and the things I had told him, he stilled loved me. He pushed through the muddy and dirty spots in my life to see me free at the end.

As I began meeting with him on a regular basis it became easier for me to see truth in myself. He was always there to encourage me and pick me up when I was down, just to direct me back to the one that changed me in the first place. Jesus. I really saw that he not only lived a life in order to help others but he lived a life that could be followed. Something he said to me, not only changed my view on ministry, but tore down walls and even changed how I look at my own flock... He said, "Blake, it doesn't even matter what happened in the past. I want you to know that I will always love you and will be here no matter what. There's nothing you could confess or say to me that would change my view of you or who you are to me."

These words spoken sincerely broke a lot of lies I

had believed for so long. When seeking freedom from homosexuality, drugs/alcohol, transsexuality, or really anything, its always important to find a leader that has the heart of Jesus. This is important because there are so many leaders out there that would take advantage of the situation or condemn you for having simple day to day issues, and when you have a leader that carries the heart of Jesus you are able to move out of the past and be "Ekballoed" or "forcefully sent" into your future.

Another important part to that scripture, as I mentioned earlier, is to have those brothers who run beside you. After spending the summer connecting to my mentor, I began running with two guys that would eventually be in my wedding. They had such a deep impact on me in this transitioning season that I will probably run with them for the rest of my life. I had one best friend who had also struggled with same sex-attraction and we had bonded together to run this race and finish with flying colors.

We were almost the same person so we got along for the most part, and we found that our love for the outdoors would take us to some of the most incredible places in Hamilton, AL. We would have deep talks about where we were spiritually and prayer sessions that lead us to heavenly places. I STRONGLY encourage surrounding yourself with a couple of people to be a part of what I call, "The Inner Circle." These people are those who are strong and grounded in the word as well as able to relate to where you are at spiritually. This way you can have accountability and complete trust in someone in order to make the journey a lot less lonely.

My other main partner in crime was my roommate. After living with him for a year in the house and then needing a roommate my second year, I felt like God had planned for us to live together again. We had gotten closer towards the end of my first year aside from all of our past beef and it was like a long-lasting connection was being formed without us even knowing it. That summer I began praying for him and for the finances to be given in order for him to actually come back for a second year of schooling.

That bond got stronger after hours of prayer and then by that August it was like we were brothers separated at birth. Him coming back that next year gave me assurance that God had bonded us for something greater. Throughout the year we would keep each other in check and held one another accountable. I taught him a thing or two about the world of Disney and theatre and he taught me of this foreign land they called *sports*. This particular relationship helped me not only to learn I could have brothers, but I could *be a brother*. After so much time believing the twisted lies the enemy placed in my head it was incredible to think I could be a brother!

None of the guys that helped me through this ever cared about my screw-ups or my downfalls. They helped me back on my feet and said, "Lets keep going." This real brotherhood began making sense to me and without that brotherhood I wouldn't be where I am today. Even now I continue to connect with that same leader, as I move through this journey, to get his advice or his thoughts about a situation. My two best friends will always be there, as will I for them, and no matter what.

We carry a life long bond that God has blessed us with. These three men not only taught me about brotherhood, but also helped teach me how to be a man. Different elements of manhood were being revealed to me through these three guys and I can never thank them enough for being who they are. After believing for so long that I was destined to be a woman, it was incredible to me that God could change the outcome and reset the picture.

I was growing into a man, into manhood, and over time when I would get discouraged or feel out of place, I would remember something I heard from a wise minister. He said "to be a man you don't have to like big trucks, or go fishing, or love hunting, you just have to be like the man who carries the real meaning of manhood, *Jesus.*" Since learning these things, not only have I grown to appreciate who my dad is, but I have grown to see a brother that was always next to me. My brother, by blood, and my father were always right beside me, but because I was so blinded by my own ideas and ambition I could never see that. And until I did, it made facing the giants before me difficult.

7

A FOUR-LETTER WORD: H.A.T.E

AS YOU BEGIN THIS PROCESS, as I did, you will find unfortunately that the support of those you once cherished won't be your backbone. The people that helped you come out of the closet will tell you there's not way out. That it is IMPOSSIBLE to change your mind or decide to be different. Hatred can sneak up on you, it can be blatantly thrown at you, but it seems that no matter where it comes from, or how it comes, it still hurts just as bad.

Hatred and disapproval have always been a factor in my life, because I have always been really scared of what people thought of me and how I could fix the way they perceived me. It simply caused a lot of fear and insecurity in my life that carried over into my newfound life I am living following God. Being gay and trying to find some form of acceptance from those that are so close-minded can be the hardest thing you do, but it is also hard to find acceptance when you come out of a life you never wanted.

At first I felt like someone had blinded me, and right when they take off the blindfold, I saw that I was in a pool full of sharks ready to attack at any moment. I have feared the words, daggers, and the cuts in my character, which I may encounter from making this lifestyle choice. Some have feared for me but, at this point, it's no longer a matter of what people say or how people feel, it's a matter of how God moves in a situation to change the words of death into life.

I read something recently that mentioned the heart posture of King David when he consulted with God in Psalm 80:3, "Restore us, O God; make Your face shine on us, that we may be saved." In this article it was explained that David was in such a place of hurt, he knew only God could change feelings and circumstances when it came to the human complex. Hate is a four-letter word, but each letter is just as sharp as the first dagger thrown. When hatred, bitterness or even anger get thrown at you, you must learn to not automatically shut down and cower away. You have to allow God to move in your heart in order to stay strong and move forward through the clouds. Hatred, I believe, is something that only God can extract from our hearts and replace it with His love and grace, because there are just some things only God can change in our hearts.

Proverbs 10:12 literally says, "Hatred stirs up quarrels, but love makes up for all offenses." Hatred was designed to stir up these feelings of anger, but letting go of that can allow you to see all of the other opportunities for God to work in your life. For me personally, living a life of homosexuality was really frightening when I felt I was held to certain standards. Hiding under lock and key to stay in a closet I never belonged in.

When I got out and gained freedom it became even more frightening to "go out unto the world" and tell people about my story. I was afraid of what people would say...and for awhile, the comments really did hurt. "You are full of lies," "Your life is sad," "You aren't helping anyone by lying for fame, **quit**," "What are you doing?" Those things did hurt. It made me a little scared of what was to come. It seemed that even though my message was of a loving and accepting Jesus, people heard me and thought, "Oh, just another preacher screaming GOD HATES FAGS," I never intended for that to be heard or thought. I cried so many nights because I just wanted people to hear me for what I was *really saying.*

It amazed me though, that a people group that gets bashed by so many people daily wouldn't have an ounce of love for someone who merely found unhappiness in what the world promoted as the answer. I was just looking for acceptance for my newfound heterosexual life. I found it a little ironic because it seemed as if I had been hiding it and now I had to have the conversation with loved ones, "I'm. Uhh... I'm straight." But finding acceptance from the homo and hetero community was a lot harder than it sounded. As I went to churches and ministered, or even just told my story to a majority of males, I got a reaction that after a while I came to expect. They talked about how wonderful it was that I had been changed, but then treated me like I had the flu and if they got too close to me they might contract the same illness.

Once men find out that you had a past in homosexuality, even ministers, they act as if you'll turn in to this homo-were-creature and pounce on them. I have heard 100s of testimonies on drug abuse, alcoholism, depression and even suicidal thoughts, but when a guy gets saved and delivered from homosexuality, people act as if he could turn again at any moment. Women on the other hand have just as many barriers to cross. Many of times I have heard a women's testimony about coming out of a lesbian lifestyle and it's just seen as a "sexual phase." It seems that when a girl comes out and says, "I was a lesbian and I am now free," it gets swept under the rug as "No sweetheart that was just a phase or a sexual fetish." Freedom is freedom and you can't let anyone demean your freedom.

I admit there are battles and struggles coming out of a gay/lesbian/drag lifestyle that many of you will face and gain freedom from, but there is no reason people should treat you differently than anyone else. Then it hit me. The church/world has poured so much hatred into and towards the homosexual community that why does it surprise anyone they give that hatred right back. From a gay's-eye-view, the church is ready to set fire to those who don't immediately turn from their ways, so it's no wonder people in the community want things like "gay-safe zones" in our school systems because so much hate gets pushed towards the community.

As a minister with a homosexual background, I have been told many times that *I can never really be changed and I'll still end up in hell with everyone else,* but I refuse to believe that. For me being gay, on top of all of my other issues, made me just want to die. I didn't want that life and yet I felt it chose me. Why did I have to accept it? There were so many conflicting thoughts that I couldn't handle it.

It seemed like some Christians had this view of the homosexual community as if they were lepers and they should be locked up in a community of their own so the world would be purified. This was simply ridiculous and childish thinking. In reality, whether you are coming out of a gay lifestyle or trying to understand the process, we all have to let go of the hatred and accept Jesus the way He does us. Like in Psalm 80:3, we have to let God give us the acceptance and satisfaction we desire. We have to love everyone as Jesus would and let Him do the changing. It's not about whether we are gay, alcoholic, druggies or thugs; it's all equal in God's eyes. Sin is sin and we must move past it, because God does.

Hatred can be a very dangerous weapon when coming straight out of the LGBTQ community. You must guard your heart in everything you do because people can easily come in and let the enemy convince you otherwise. You must stay strong in what God has said and not waiver from that. Just as you may have experienced the hatred when coming out of the closet, you have to be ready to brush off the negative words that are thrown at you for leaving this lifestyle you never really belonged in.

One of my best friends in ministry recently said this to me in regard to hatred, and it has truly stuck out to me. She said, "Everyone deserves redemption. Freedom is freely given, that is the purpose of the cross. Every person has a story and sin nature. It may all look different but it is all equal in the eyes of the King. Everyone's story deserves to be heard and celebrated and encouraged. Bringing it to the light expels the darkness!" This inspires me, as it should everyone. Everyone deserves a chance, a moment, *a freeing eureka!* Allow the mind frames of the past to fade away, and let God show you how to take the steps that are necessary to a transition such as this.

Although there is still hatred in the darkness out there, there is a whole community of love out there for the people that come out of this lifestyle. I have only

FROM MASCARA TO MANHOOD   43

recently discovered a large and vast community of people who are like me. Communities of people that are running full force after God and that have successfully left the cage they locked themselves in. Through this revelation of God being bigger than hatred you realize...*love wins*.

8

A DECISION TO LOVE

AS I JUST MENTIONED BEFORE there is a whole community out there for those who are trying to find freedom from homosexuality. There are tons of people daily coming out of this lifestyle to run after God that can be a help to you in your transition. I have always believed that this change wasn't just "gay to straight" but "broken to whole." For those of you with same sex attraction, whether you are a minister, a follower of Jesus, or simply an unbeliever, this is a simple truth you must grasp in order to understand this transition. This is not a situation where you magically become straight, but a heart posture the Holy Spirit brings you to, not only to be right with God but to turn from your fleshly desires because you love Him more.

Genesis talks about Eve being deceived by the serpent, and how he convinced her that by not eating the fruit she had been told not to eat, she was *missing out* and *God was holding something back from her.* This battle, for many people, comes up often, especially in the gay community. People feel like God is holding back something from them. Instead of listening to what He said, they take what they feel they deserve and ignore God's divine plan for them. God said: *You may freely eat the fruit of every tree in the garden—except the tree of the knowledge of good and evil. If you eat its fruit, you are sure to die.* It looks desirable because it is mysterious and you may fantasize about it, but "You are sure to die!"

Now obviously you won't actually die, but you fall from everything God had in store for you. The first lie told in the garden was that the Father was hiding something from His kids and now we must take back what is rightfully ours, but in reality God never hid a thing. He told us what would happen, and gave us a warning label. He simply was protecting us from something that could damage everything he made for us. He isn't a taker or thief, He is a provider, He is truth; and He is constantly calling us back to Him.

This journey I went on, I keep referring to it as a "transition," but it was not only a transition, it was also *a decision to love.* Not only did Jesus die for us, but He lived for us too! Jesus understood the human complex enough to sacrifice Himself for our sins so no matter what, we could be made whole. This was a decision to love. I also made that decision to love Him. I fell in love with Him and had to decide that because of that, I wouldn't act on my fleshly desires. It's not about going from gay to straight but it's about being made holy and through the strength of God not acting on our temptations.

Throughout the Bible, God always makes the decision to love. He always decides to move past what the world called us and show us love. Jonah was made a perfect example of God's love. In the Book of Jonah God chooses to love Jonah through his disobedience and his destruction just to be with him. God loved Jonah. As the story of Jonah and the whale unfolds, Jonah is asked by God to go to Nineveh and prophesy impending judgment due to their breaking of God's commandments. Jonah immediately freaks out and flees the scene, as many people do when they feel like they are being pressed to change. Jonah jumps on the next departing boat and sails across the ocean.

During the boat ride, God comes to the location of the boat with a storm to wake Jonah up. For many of us this is a wake up call we need to push us to the next step. Now this storm makes many think God was angry with Jonah and that He was punishing him until he changed his mind, but I feel differently. God showed me that this was an act of desperation to truly show Jonah His love and that He would do anything for him. The other crew members wake Jonah from his nap and tell him to pray to whichever god he believes in, to save them from this storm. He then explains that he is the reason the God of the heavens has brought this storm and tells them if they throw him overboard the storm will stop.

If we would just stop and realize that God is just trying to get our attention we could truly see the love He has for us. After the crew throw him overboard the storm ceases and because the crew sees this, they immediately begin worshiping the true God. Some translations say, "They were awestruck by the Lord's great power and LOVE, they offered a sacrifice and vowed to serve God." A whale then swallows Jonah, and Jonah stays in its belly for three days and three nights. In that time he is in the belly of the whale I thought, "Why a whale, why not a raft?"

God then showed me that although He will climb mountains and cross seas for us He would also do absolutely anything just to commune with us. God showed me that in that time Jonah was able to realign with God and spend time with his Father who loved him so much. God will do the same for you. God will chase you across an ocean to get you alone to just hang out with you and to love on you. Personally I felt if someone is willing to do all of that just for me I must have something for Him in return. I chose to love God, and because I did, He gave me the strength to turn from my old ways and live a life that is holy and worthy.

The way the world moves now, everything seems to boil down to sexuality. Personally this isn't about sexuality or even about us, but it is the love of God changing our motives and our hearts to make us who He created us to be. This is not only a change and a transition, but it is a journey of realizing love always wins. I have heard so many stories from guys and girls that live in a homosexual lifestyle that say "I had a conservative upbringing and being gay wasn't an option, so I didn't want to be a part of a God who didn't want love and happiness for me."

I ask them if they have ever *pursued God,* outside of their family traditions. Every time I've gotten the answer "...No." So how are you so sure He is all of these things you believed? When you actually seek God alone, without considering what your family says, and when you are truly just getting to know *Him*, you will see the lies you once believed melt away and you will find a God who is loving and caring and ready to accept you in His arms. So yes. *Love always wins.*

9

WHAT IS THIS FEELING?

IN MY LIFE, as I shared with you before, I had always dreamed of being married. Married to someone that I could share my life with. I wanted someone to share my dreams with, my wants, my home and so much more than that. Being that I had only been attracted to guys ever since I could remember, it was hard to see marriage any other way. Even with my relationship with Jesus, I still couldn't see myself being attracted to a girl. I knew that it was what God intended for me, but I couldn't force how I felt and I didn't want to have to settle for something that wouldn't satisfy me fully in every area. Another thought that haunted my mind was "who could marry a guy like me?"

After all the men I had slept with and the things I had done, how could any woman take me the way I was? How could anyone be OK with the fact that I had only been with guys and forced myself to date girls. How could they not live in constant fear I would go back to a guy at any moment? Now you may be thinking, *this is where he tells us he realized being straight wasn't an option, so he settled for celibacy,* but *no, I didn't settle.* Although I call it a transition, which it was, and I no longer considered myself a part of the LGBTQ community, the transition between being attracted to men and being attracted to women just didn't exist.

Yes, God's love is real. Yes, God's mercy and strength are real, but coming out of a gay lifestyle is also real. When I went out, I never experienced a time that I could look at a girl and think "I could take HER right now." I wanted to believe that if God wanted me to be with a women He would show me how to desire her. As I have previously mentioned, I had to guard my mind, so when I saw that chiseled jaw and smelled fresh cologne, I didn't think "I want HIM to take me right now." Every point and piece of advice I have given are still valid and I needed all of those things when I was going through this transition, but the transition wasn't over yet.

Here's where *hope* truly became a reality. As my second year of ministry school was really taking off, I met someone who pushed me to keep seeking more of God and showed me that love outside of guys was real. This girl's name was Anissa. As Anissa and I began to become friends, we began to see and realize that our stories were more alike than we thought. You see before heading to ministry school, Anissa was in a LESBIAN relationship. It was a miracle! I had found someone that was not only an ex member of the LGBTQ community, but was someone who related to all of my feelings! It was insane. She had been with guys and girls, but before experiencing God in a REAL way she had made plans to celebrate our nation's new freedom of marriage with tying the knot with her girlfriend.

She unfolded more and more of her story, and we began to grow together. We held each other accountable and decided to take this journey of growing as best friends. We continued in this process together and it soon became clear that there might be more. Then it began. One day we were riding home from work, as we had to work in a city 40 miles away from school to make any real money, and we began praying. Not about anything in particular, we just wanted to hear the voice of God. Then I heard myself say, in my head, *I could do this with her forever.* I opened my eyes immediately. I was shocked. Was I? Could I? Am I attracted to a girl? It couldn't be. Every relationship up until this point I had felt like I forced the attraction. It was just "supposed to be that way" because I was an "ex-gay," but no, I was actually attracted to her. Her laugh, her smile, her eyes, her love for God, all of these things among many others caused me to be drawn to her.

I still wasn't attracted to girls as a whole but I was attracted to *her.* This was a concept that I wasn't familiar with yet. Days and weeks passed and I thought that all of this was nothing but a long dream I was in that I hadn't woken up from. Then as the weeks passed I thought, "Okay, so *amen* you're attracted to a girl. This girl is also a little older than you and she knows your sexual history…she won't be into you like that…" I shut myself down before I gave it a shot.

The Lord had done this amazing thing, but I was just too scared to risk it all crashing down. Months pass and we traveled to work as normal, but this time she says to me "I need to tell you something" when she gets in the car. We go and pick up our other carpool buddy and she leaves me wondering what this "something" is for the rest of the evening. After dropping our friend off and heading to her dorm to drop her off, we began discussing the details of a text she had sent me after work that night, but before we made it back home. "I have feelings for someone and it might be you." Yes, she actually *liked me.*

After discussing our feelings and realizing we could be the one for each other, we decided to give dating a try. As time progressed and one month turned into one year I found myself absolutely head over heels for this girl, Anissa, and I asked her to marry me. What is this feeling? Happiness. Wholeness. Bliss. *God?* That's what it was, *God!* Am I sexually attracted to women, as a whole? No. However, I am attracted to Anissa. Not because I fasted and prayed the gay away, not because I was taken to the Third Heaven and purified by the lightning hand of God, but because God fashioned Anissa with my prayers and qualities in mind.

She knows my sexual history, she knows where I have been, she knows my crazy stories and my little quirks but yet she still loves me anyway. With her I never had to worry about how much to show and how much to hold back. From the beginning we became best friends who told each other everything. We grew on a foundation of truth and not false perceptions of who the other person might be. She loves me like Jesus does and so why shouldn't I love her the same way.

10

MORALITY OVER SEXUALITY

THE IDEA that there is just one way of doing this is absolutely preposterous. Every person who has struggled with homosexuality, that I have encountered, have all had a different process, though one thing can be agreed on. Jesus. Jesus was the answer and Jesus was the key that changed everything. Although morality is black and white, with this particular subject people can get lost sometimes deciphering what's black and what's white. For me it is simple.

I know what is considered lust in my head, I know my boundaries and I know the triggers that can make me think unholy thoughts. At the end of the day whether you are someone looking to transition, a believer just looking for knowledge on the subject, or you have successfully transitioned, the one thing to remember is that this whole thing is about a relationship. It's about

God who just wants to be your Father and you have to decide what comes between you and Him. If I had chosen to leave everything God had given me, and pursued a man, I would have thrown away the hopes and dreams I have created in my new life. I would not only have thrown away the relationships and bonds I've created, but I would be giving up a chance to have a heavenly Father who cares for me more than I can fully understand.

It is me, choosing to give up everything I have and telling God that this boy I'm after, is more important than Him or anything He could give me. This grieves me so much and I think, after everything God has shown me, after everything I have done with God, how could I even consider going back. Looking back at everything that has happened in my life leading to this point, I wouldn't change a thing. I think the biggest thing that people who disagree with my choice to transition out of a homosexual lifestyle forget to ask is, "Are you happy?"

People are so quick to call it "fake," "brainwashed," "sad," "not legit," yet they never seem to consider that this entire decision was mine from the beginning. Some who experience me now may still say "He's still gay, you can't just pray the gay away..." but the one thing they never think about is that when I made this decision, I made it thinking I would just go right back to my boyfriend and live happily ever after. When I encountered God, I realized that nothing that this world had for me could satisfy me. On top of leaving the boys behind, I left my drugs and alcoholic habits. I left behind everything I thought I knew about God and the world and discovered something brand new. He gave me *restoration*.

11

THE RESTORATION OF THE RAINBOW

Genesis 9:12-16 (NLT) "Then God said, 'I am giving you a sign of my covenant with you and with all living creatures, for all generations to come. I have placed my rainbow in the clouds. It is the sign of my covenant with you and with all the earth. When I send clouds over the earth, the rainbow will appear in the clouds, and I will remember my covenant with you and with all living creatures.'"

THE RAINBOW FLAG. The biggest symbol of gay pride. One of the biggest things that I have noticed and reminded everyone of over the years is that the "Pride Flag" is not a complete rainbow. You see man just had to come up with something that appears to be amazing, but when you really look at it, it's not complete. God created the rainbow from the beginning to be a symbol of His promise. A covenant with man that God would never bring destruction, but preserve the life He created and to continuously remind man of that truth. He sets the rainbow upon the clouds to show us, He is near, He loves us, and He longs for His creation to love Him.

Through my journey the love and acceptance of Jesus was the only acceptance I needed to fill my void. I went through so many stages and phases with God and so will you. If you are starting, continuing or even thinking about this journey, you have to hold onto the promise. That Jesus is bigger than same sex attraction. He has given us a freedom that we can actually obtain. The 7 colors in the rainbow, red, yellow, green, orange, blue, indigo, and violet, all represent a piece of the PERFECT promise God has given us. I believe God is "Restoring the Rainbow" and putting back the seventh color the world could never have mimicked. The 6 color rainbow is only part of what God has for us, so why settle for less when we can have EVERYTHING.

God restored my rainbow. I now have my wife, my father, my brother, my family, my sexuality, my freedom and future. All because I took a chance and stepped out of the closet. I pray that this book blesses you. I pray that you related to my story and could find yourself in it somewhere. God is moving in this community and He is bringing His perfect love in to cover everything we have carried. Let go of the brokenness. Let go of the hurt. Let down the walls. When you do, God will color your world like you could never have imagined. He will take you on an endless adventure that continues to get better and better.

Church, take heed to the advice I have given. Stand up for what is right, but stand in love while doing it. Remember what God has said and hold onto that promise. The rainbow isn't just for the people that have gained freedom, but it is also placed in the sky to remind you, there is *hope*. There is hope for the loved one that is trapped in what the world calls "freedom." Hold tight to your word and when you do, things will change. You may think it's just getting worse. It's just too hard. You miss them too much. You just want them back, but when God makes a promise to bring freedom. He does.

> Ephesians 1:5 (ESV) "He predestined us for adoption to himself as sons through Jesus Christ, according to the purpose of his will."

As the title suggests, this is a true story of a transition, and as the scriptures suggest, it's about identity. It is an ongoing story about a man that transitions from mascara, to manhood...*and is now free.*

MEET THE AUTHOR

Benjamin Howard is in full time ministry with his wife Anissa. Although Benjamin and his wife love ministering in the LGBTQ community, his focus is primarily on teens in the youth group they lead at Xtreme Harvest Church in San Antonio. Benjamin Howard and his wife have both been set free from homosexuality and want to see thousands find the truth and light they have experienced. They have two dogs, Walter Elias and Lillian Marie and they reside in San Antonio, Texas.

INDIVIDUAL COPIES OF

FROM MASCARA TO MANHOOD

CAN BE ORDERED AT:

OR

*BULK ORDERS/RATES CAN BE FOUND AT:

TALLPINEBOOKS.COM

Made in the USA
Columbia, SC
18 March 2024

33242805R00048